THE UNFOLLOWING

Previous Books

Poetry

My Life and My Life in the Nineties (Wesleyan University Press, 2013)
The Book of a Thousand Eyes (Omnidawn Books, 2012)
The Wide Road (with Carla Harryman; Belladonna, 2010)
Saga / Circus (Omnidawn Books, 2008)
Situations, Sings (with Jack Collom; Adventures in Poetry, 2008)
The Lake (with Emilie Clark; Granary Books, 2004)
The Fatalist (Omnidawn Books, 2003)
Slowly (Tuumba Press, 2002)
A Border Comedy (Granary Books, 2001)
The Beginner (Spectacular Books, 2000; Tuumba Press, 2002)
Happily (Post-Apollo Press, 2000)
Chartings (with Ray Di Palma; Chax Press, 2000)
Sight (with Leslie Scalapino; Edge Books, 1999)
The Traveler and the Hill and the Hill (mixed media; with Emilie Clark; Granary Books, 1998)
The Cold of Poetry (Sun & Moon Press, 1994)
The Cell (Sun & Moon Press, 1992)
Oxota: A Short Russian Novel (The Figures, 1991)
Individuals (with Kit Robinson; Chax Press, 1988)
Writing is an Aid to Memory (The Figures, 1978; reprinted by Sun & Moon, 1996)
A Mask of Motion (Burning Deck, 1977)

Critical Prose

The Grand Piano: An Experiment in Collective Autobiography,
(with Rae Armantrout, Steve Benson, Carla Harryman, Tom Mandel,
Ted Pearson, Bob Perelman, Kit Robinson, Ron Silliman, and Barrett Watten;
Mode A, 2006–2009)
The Language of Inquiry (University of California Press, 2000)
Leningrad (with Michael Davidson, Ron Silliman, Barrett Watten;
Mercury House, 1991)

THE UNFOLLOWING

LYN HEJINIAN

OMNIDAWN PUBLISHING
OAKLAND, CALIFORNIA
2016

Cover art by Sofie Ramos ©2015
www.sofieramos.com.

Cover and interior design by Cassandra Smith

Library of Congress Cataloging-in-Publication Data

Names: Hejinian, Lyn, author.
Title: The unfollowing / Lyn Hejinian.
Description: Oakland, California : Omnidawn Publishing, [2016]
Identifiers: LCCN 2015040551 | ISBN 9781632430151 (softcover : acid-free
  paper)
Classification: LCC PS3558.E4735 A6 2016 | DDC 811/.54--dc23
LC record available at http://lccn.loc.gov/2015040551

Published by Omnidawn Publishing, Oakland, California
www.omnidawn.com   (510) 237-5472   (800) 792-4957
10 9 8 7 6 5 4 3 2 1
ISBN: 978-1-63243-015-1

Acknowledgements

A number of these poems have been published in the following literary journals, sometimes in earlier versions: *Aerial* (in a special issue dedicated to the author's work, edited by Jen Hofer and Rod Smith); the *Berkeley Poetry Review* 2004 and 2008 (thanks to Danni Gordon, Andrew David King, Julia Wood, and Noor al-Samarrai); *Coconut* (thanks to Bruce Covey); the *Colorado Review* (thanks to Dan Beachy-Quick and Sasha Steensen); *Court Green* (the poetry journal of Columbia College Chicago); *Hambone* (thanks to Nathaniel Mackey); *Hysteria* (a feminist journal published at the School of Oriental and African Studies, University of London; thanks to Bjørk Grue Lidin); *Jelly Bucket* (thanks to Lisa Schmidley); *Lana Turner* (thanks to David Lau and Calvin Bedient); *La Volta* (thanks to Joshua Marie Wilkinson); *Shiny* (thanks to Michael Fried); *Zoland* (thanks to Cris Mattison). The sequence of poems that appeared in *Lana Turner* was later included in *Pushcart Prize XXXIX: Best of the Small Presses* (and I thank Bill Henderson and the poetry editors of that volume for this).

A small group of poems was published as a chapbook by the Kavyayantra Press at Naropa University; thanks to Julia Seko.

Daniel Cuesta, editor of washing machine press, brought out a very limited-edition chapbook of three of the poems; my thanks to him.

Squircle Line Press published a broadside of poem 7 (thanks to Desmond Kon Xicheng-Minde).

Poem 57 appeared on the Academy of American Poets "Poem-a-Day" website in the spring of 2013; poem 60 appeared on the same website in April, 2015. Both occasions were curated by Alex Dimitrov; thank you.

In memoriam
Charlotte Ehrengard Ellertson
March 2, 1966-March 21, 2004

and the others
lost from life

Preface

An attentive, or perhaps merely line-counting, reader will come fairly quickly to the conclusion that "The Unfollowing" is a set, if not a sequence, of sonnets. This wouldn't be inaccurate—or it would be entirely so. The poems are all fourteen lines long, and I did most certainly have the sonnet in mind when I decided to adhere to a fourteen-line constraint. But at the conclusion of a proper sonnet, regardless of whatever residual ambiguities remain, something like a resolution is achieved. Sonnets are the summit of logicality. The sonnet proper develops argumentatively, unfolding under the pressure of reasons appropriate to whatever problem or situation it is exploring. The "Unfollowing" poems do not. They are intended to be illogical.

That they would be so was, I thought, guaranteed by another, and more important, feature of their structure. The fourteen-line constraint was not the only one I imposed on the making of the poems. I also required myself to build them with non-sequiturs. Nothing was to follow—or nothing follow logically. I wanted each line to be as difficult to accept on the basis of the previous and subsequent lines as death is for we who are alive—a comparison that I make intentionally, since my intention in writing the sequence of poems I'm calling "The Unfollowing" was to compose a set of elegies.

The initial occasion for mourning was a personal one, the death, from cancer, of a young member of my immediate family. That death overturned whatever "logic" I had trusted to prevail over the larger patterns of the familiar world and over the details and particulars through which we experience it on a daily basis, the logic whereby living makes sense. But in the time since her death (now seven years ago), there has been much to mourn in the public sphere, too. Indeed, there is ample cause in the world for real political anguish and justifiable cosmic despair. Whatever checks on capitalism's rapacity existed (or perhaps only seemed to exist) even a decade ago are all but non-existent now. More and more brazenly, capitalism commits crimes against humanity. And, indeed, it isn't only, and not even primarily, humanity that is suffering. These are truly sad times, even for sparrows and ragweed.

The illogical, unstabilizable form of my elegiac response to the death of a young woman was intended to express my sense of that death's unacceptability. I did not, as I began writing the "Unfollowing" poems, have any way to foresee how much more would come along that was also, and in many ways more, unacceptable.

I did foresee that some parts of the poems would be funny, however. Laughter and weeping are not so very different from each other. And if logic can't prevail, perhaps hilarity can, as an attribute of a revolutionary practice of everyday life, dismantling control and reforming connectivity.

Poems can't achieve all this, of course—perhaps not even any of it.

1

The spy unfolds his hammock and creates in effect an enormous basket into
        which he tumbles, wobbles, and comes to rest like a freshly laid mottled
        yellow egg
The fog has rolled in, visibility is null, I wouldn't know if someone were
        following me
A woman throws beans, a woman rakes leaves, a heavy man moves ahead on
        a horse, a light man coughs
The visible is rough
There are all kinds of words here and some that aren't here and some that
        might if put together in the right order mean more to you than I
        can say
It seems that it's lighter or maybe just browner
Today—what kind of beginning is that, what kind of end
The streets are walked by she who fully backwards walks them emptily
O nomad, come here, O death, rest your head
Eleven lines may be woven with three into an elegy, an entropy, a
        velocipede, a punishment, and a pin
Let's go, across the fields far from here, lunch finished, no further discussion
        arising, to climb the sheer rock face now that the fruits on the tree
        atop it are ripe
A little cloud obscures the sun, then dissipates and the sun's begun
There was once an old woman with cake on her face, there was once an old
        man dressed all in black lace
We will receive (do receive / are receiving / have received / have to receive
        / will have received / won't receive / shall receive) a young
        Argentinean captain

2

Every minute proves that reality is conditional
Sounds paddle the air echoing when I speak my mind
The door opens, I rise naked from the tub
It's strange to return to Abyssinia by train from my bed
I hear a demographer singing below
Sleep?—yes, I sleep in fear almost of the lovely night before I slept
Boom—one—one—one, boom one and boom one and one and one
Only one
A woman appears carrying a pink bag
You stay, okay with the sheets, we'll get a suit, you're in the story
When love can't be composed any better, then love can't be postponed any longer
Things predicted are always restricted
Go, smoking pan, with your bacon to window
This afternoon there will be "une grande séance" and everyone will nap

3

All that the girl thought irrelevant was never to become relevant to her

At the far left in the upper corner we can see the "Blessed Islands," at the
bottom to the right it says "The End"

I am horrified, he has been shot, I see the blood on his hands and head, but now
I see that the victim isn't who I thought it was, he has turned to beseech
me but it's just some blond stranger—I don't care a bit about him and
walk away

Time's retraction brings the failure of action

Elbow, richness, auburn, critic, water rising through the plumbing system

Anomalies cannot provide

No dummies, they were experiencing, then experience ceased

A scream from within a circle of chairs, an ascending of stairs, and then the
scream's cancellation—all accomplished without any screaming

A sphinx, a grid, and a cyclist in red

It was a warm day, March 8, the co-ed had sweat on her lip, a foretaste of spring

Knowledge is lost in redundant unexpectedness

A field, a flash of emergence, the present, new ideals

A moan

An elf with so many toes on her feet, bam bam, that she couldn't wear boots,
dam dam, stepped into hot coals, ram ram

4

One spring the wise guys booming *one* paraded: boom: 1
The next thing they knew, it was a warm day in spring, and each had several
      deaths to mourn
Is this another sphinx trick, a hole, a minus-device like a mad wave
Up go the shades, but there's no light outside to be let in
She concentrated for, she identified in, she told to
They who accomplish banging gather, they who diminish do so proudly
Half is done with a quarter to spend by a worrywart wearing sunglasses
The sun is too coherent, the egg in the glacier hatches out mice
Mother!
As generous as a caterpillar she has given her very body away
Now we witness with the senses and materiality is singled out
Mad manifest squares, the semantics of an evil activity
The phrase, this stream, among wolves
How vulgar the vulnerability of the earholes, the armholes—of anything that
      serves as a window of the body to the world

5

A drowned or drowning baby is being dragged up through the lake by one foot,
     scales of sound still to study
Predicate without prepositions, subject supposedly shown
Everywhere manifestation, nowhere explanation
"Across the wide rivers," "a stranger has robbed them," "send for my dog"
You can't at first sight discern that a metamorphosis is underway
Bluntly the pointless pointer rubs, the best bits blown
Along comes the surgeon who cannot unwound the soldier in an epic known by
     the names of the nations that have fought for the tools with which the dirt
     is being thrown into his grave
Think of it: Hamlet driven mad by the political success of the profoundly undeserving
Rice along, sleep appearance, tether mother twin as true bugs, cogitate
The sounds depart from their sources and arrive to warn us that their sources are near
She's had/will have no leaning with the orange in it of it
Joe says the blushing sun has set, Jane says Napoleon slept in fits, and Henry says
     his siblings are all hippopotami, dour and grey
They say that nature never jumps but nature does
Some—the sung—the sun

6

The day comes up from a severed page
Joe has standing whiskers, Jane has a secret
The dancer is ballooning, he's fat and light-footed, he's becoming airborne,
      nothing's in his way
How oppressed the young woman is by her mother's image of the happiness that
      must be hers
Along comes a wave casting spray as it bears—down on a man half-asleep on a
      towel and half-awake in a rowboat adrift on a violent sea
The cold in this luminous season stings
Let us go then, you and I, in pajamas through the sky, in which we'll dine on
      rice and pie, we'll drink from apples made of lace, we'll topple statues,
      invent space
There in her hand is a slice of bread, its surface just beginning to stiffen
Can we question this
The stars are bits of fire that have broken off from earth
Like ants we must make our choices quickly
Death we cannot people, lens, clock, or declare
Thunder here is rare, no matter how thick the air with things with sides to
      strike into view
Time's flow is dammed and the past comes back

7

To begin with, I am faced with mountains to circumambulate, since I can't cut
     through them
I enter the folds of a human adventure
On every door there hangs a figurehead and this one comes to face me as the
     door swings shut
I will proceed with good will—the best of wills—anxiously
Bird of daughters, bird flying from the forks, the blurbs, the serials, the time
I saw a golden tadpole, eating apple jam; I saw a sudden whirlpool, sucking
     down a ham
The boughs groan with fruit, an apple falls—false alarm
It's a non-sequitur—that
Sense data sinks
The muscles give out mid-word and a thief stutters while accusing me (his
     uncle) of theft
Lune comes along mounted on a beast called That who is neither more nor less
     than a horse as obedient to Lune as the tides are to the moon
Shot of men hurrying toward each other at an intersection with open umbrellas
     none willing to give way to the others, shot of placid camels kneeling near
     a chained dog, shot of sugar maples temporarily obscured by falling snow
Tomorrow morning, unless things vastly improve, I'll go in person to the front
     of the caravan and take it *over* the mountain
I thought I saw an earthworm, stirring in the dirt, then I saw it was a sadist,
     wielding a quirt

8

There goes something, forever lost in context
A Sudanese customs agent halts a caravan carrying rocking chairs into lands
      where no rocking chairs are needed
Come lest desire clatter, dance now lest we can't dance later
Here remains as a bridge vanishes, the backdoor shuts, etc., and here cares little as
      to which is which
Conjoining unlike concepts (say, birth control and origami) is something mortals do
This does not follow
Window a red chocolate, melon in a tumult, stone of clouded jazz, milk a
      penciled elephant—all in a row
The passengers on prison ships are not allowed to celebrate
There is very little, almost nothing, that …
I order you to feel free to help yourself to ice cream which is melting
At midnight I'll become a merchant mariner again
Is this paper snow, undertow
It is perceived unconsciously and might have been a spider emerging from a
      duck's egg, a cause for excitement provided by the outside world to an
      inner world that almost missed it
It's only with clumsy freedom that things appear on people's lips

9

Smoke is the noun for the thing over the fire, to sting is the verb for what's
      being done
It is only in *this* light that I can see the spider's web
Along comes a girl with mighty thighs astride an equine butter
Nothing rises that doesn't rise
A woman had the finer python and its name was Palm but she called it Call
A blown shell
New consonants are discovered far more often than they can be used
Come rain or shine, *she* takes the umbrella on even days of the month and *she*
      takes it on odd, and whomever the dog loves best, it will follow
Gone is the adjective *lost*—or was it *last*
In the Museum called Unless hangs the pelt of a beast that seldom comes to hand
That's all
Can we call life falling
We can talk to each other about tiles, snowballs, and camels
In a cave of ice—while wild weather rages outside—she—anticipating the loss
      of her crown—makes a comment, opposed by none

10

Late at night the insects sing it
Stories do not float
Should maples shade the growing grass, some will pause and some will pass
The killer has left a footprint on the windowsill to make everyone think he's departed
Once I went to India, in search of grand seduction, next I went to Manchester,
        with spinners, for production
Perhaps leaves fire
Is it prevented
Each elegy continues
The tree is exactly itself in its accidents
Night on our faces (for we have many) hides from us (there are many of us) our
        fates (we have many of those too)
A viola yields but could she handle it or did she hide it
The world says get out with definition
It did it did it did it
Turning everywhere in unkempt directions we must make now a new beginning

11

Who would perish stronger does and leaves us on the slope some tree or other remnant
Reason what of flurry, what of fishes, of fury
This that the body does is unlikely
The wan ants go along and go along through the woods and over the log onto leaves
       that fall into the creek where some ants drown and some ants travel
We can only ask as like to unlike ever since
There once was a woman who was allergic to cats and never allergic to eagles
What remains we ask impossibly to bother for
My daughter can speak!
It was said long ago that the stars write the sky, it was said that what enters a
       cloud will exit elsewhere
In the snapshot we find one we find absent
Ask what of fire, fever, sugar, and lag time
Papa, papa, have you come back home
In the form of a queen, the free fish returns his long lost hook to a poor fisherman
And so we see that the here and now that are constantly changing are always
       current—or are they

12

Lids cease moving and experiences fold

The pirouetting motes (saying nothing of themselves but proving that there's
air and that it moves them—they do say that much) seem little but a
light invention in the dark that keeps the world away

Closely written pages litter the tale of the avenue along which the woman
doesn't return

Is there any salt, we wonder

Call those clarifying darkroom flickers of a winged thing reasoning flurry

What upright strictly switched such shadow

Hands at her cheeks, lips parted and tip of the tongue just brushing the pink
ridge behind the teeth, she is part way through the word

It's getting harder to accept the whole tamale

Two small girls pad by the bungalow and the older one declares

We come to the often open, the pond

It's widely known that a *monstar* is a magical creature, a haunting figure, a
celestial giant, a twinkling beast

A scene is setting

Hundreds remember this

A woodpecker of wood fastened to a piece of wood by a wire and string pecks
when the string is pulled

13

Floating to earth holding onto an inflated condom down comes a swinging mouse which
        may well be an irreverent owl, a statistical pinecone, or a vestige of melancholy
The hawk, when interrupted, will metamorphose
The woman in the photograph is not to be confused with those she put at a
        distance and then brought back singly
Some say the stars are burning leaves
The truest story is a short one told "at length" and "step by step" though "all in
        vain," "all in fun," and "just for your sake"
We could stop here for the unframing, the vague resemblance, the blurring of vision
Her name was Kick, her name was also Crawl
This is full of inexplicable consonants
Between poles lie fallen wires the barbs are melting into
We want a wind that can justify the rattling of the door, the wafting of the scrap
        twisted inward away from danger
For no apparent reason, the empty sleeves of the gray wool coat that has hung in place
        for days from a sturdy hook by the door uncannily shift and the coat falls
Perhaps the books should be sealed—perhaps they should be dipped into clear
        glue or resin
Along comes a herdsmen with camels over the plains in a plan that can't be filled
She is at the tile crossroads of the fountain still

14

Citizens, the clerk announces: an interview!
It's remarkable how often one types *the* instead of *to* but it carries no more
meaning than there is to be found in the act of cutting through a large
head of cabbage
There is nobody of any importance there nor anybody of no importance
Discover the millipedes
A boy skates by, dogs leap from a bus, and then I cry "stop!"
The dog's name is Reprisal, the cat is called Ball
Glass in hand, paper plate on grass, chair over shadow, children to the left, army
approaching under cover of night
She will know nothing of what happens next
What we're watching reaches its greatest height when we're down to the last
foot of kite string
A stranger walking readily toward us appears
When this truly becomes obvious—when it is incontrovertibly true—dap dat-a-
dong, dat-a-dang, dap-a-dong
This is no way to translate, as if muzzled by the yarn binding the tongue
Behind the mask that represents the clown's lowly status the clown conceals her
lowly status
She lowers owlets into your arms as if they weren't complete without them

15

On tiptoe and mordant, trailing festival cloth, there goes a reveler with a treasure
Let us state that kindness can be easily confused with cowardice often enough
      merely to state bewilderment
If I mumble will I taunt him, will I haunt him
Less than half the gray frayed moon stays in the dark of Daylight Street still in
      the standing breeze
Under the thinking stars, blowing tequila through a drinking straw, on the
      plains of cobalt silence, of necessity we dream of necessity
Who has the plagiary, she asks
It's a fine recording, with no hisses
A paradox is not the same as scorn, contempt, or sourness, but is on the contrary
      a key component of our soulful existence
The train is in fact a curtain air can turn
This is what the consort says of knotted thoughts shot through with unshared views
It will call for a paleontologist
Jollity, sorrow, gloom, gentleness, and success appear without excuse, like a
      lunatic's opinions, and just as with a nut's ideas, randomly disappear
We conclude by promptly grafting apples
We cannot hope to continue indefinitely without ever getting into trouble

16

Air can turn rocks into ducks
Floating right up to the fence come the vast black crashing cattle, snorting
Round and narrow the warble, the arrow, the strand of very pink thread
I haven't an obligation, nor a rabbit, nor a ton of garbage
The mower draws a flower
Fatigue in horse time, horse space—oooh! tell me, liar of the moment, where's
      the barn
Time has no respect for things done without it
Two roses in the dark, one black and the other invisible
How do sentences do this?
My home is under green—who am I
The pimpled sheep-dice bear the telltale sheep tree-eyes
The piano hears a blind man
From there I push dire to pepper
Then after the fog comes a warming of fern fronds each emitting a tiny whistle

17

The sky above is blue today—but not very blue
She's been knocking marbles around in the mouth, rolling them along the teeth,
        pulling them back with the tongue
She was one who would refuse to be misled by bad data
E appears more often than T, T more often than A, A more often than I
And the tiny gray garden spiders no bigger than a grain of sand with a bright
        dot of yellow on the back and white knobs to their antennae, the
        earthworms that emerge
Man train seeks where she alights
There is nothing to prevent
Just as it is possible for A to attach to B so it is possible for C to attach to D
The one runs into the sea, the other runs from it
The older says seven avocados are needed for guacamole
Heart (absolute), readers (several), water (acts), another (recognized), view (dash)
Whatever happened to the fugue in the chimney or the clock in the chocolate
A landscape has endless false endings
A cistern of water is hidden under the yard of my daughters—who am I

18

Mother, I *like* being married

While a father attends to the cleaning of the tiles, a mother feeds blue candies to a
baby

Who taught *you* to use the word palomino, or pitch, or palimpsest, properly

A boy of 9 or 10 sits mournfully in an open field awaiting the return of his
grandfather, or perhaps he is only pretending to wait—there are tears on
his cheeks but the way he moves his feet suggests that the weeping may be
a sham meant to fool the police (who do not appear to be suspicious and
have not yet appeared)

There are two elites that rarely meet and they are the hoity-toity and the artsy-fartsy

The only elephant in sight is calmer

Riddle the floor, riddle the rock, riddle the world, riddle thrice with dice—a seven

She cannot toast, she cannot drive, certainly she can't complain

The captain's wife is rearranging the pink plastic flamingos in the rigging

Let's begin, but I can already promise that we will find more words that begin
with B than end with it

For people who rarely leave home except to go dog sledding, the sound of a
strange man singing over peaches in the market can be alarming, and it is
just such a sound that we hear now

Which way did she go, friend

That may be a wet stone but it may be a lame black horse, a dish of ink, or a crow

I'll just fold the page that the wind is coming through

19

Ten platoons of dragon-slayers step quickly forth from Fort Crooked
Good night, says the goose, at the crack of dawn
The world of the dead is past pretext, without subtext, beyond context
Shove pulls Push
That's the dream exactly as I remember it, I couldn't change a word of it now
        even if I wanted to
Do you see the surprise poplars, sense the certain sea scents too
Reality so forth drives silences that cause it thought
O dear, she put toe to ash without Simon's say so
Cold spreads like sawdust over an abandoned playground, heat like bathroom
        jokes among the children coming to play there
Far ringing air, air foreign, air faring
She was burned by an untamed flame, she lost her way in an uncommanded land
Violists, immigrants, guinea pigs—unite
If you can answer *that* riddle, you can join in the fun
Tomorrow is another day—try again: a triolet

20

Wake up, get married, be born

First A and B pick up the trunk, then C relieves A and A wanders off, then D
    takes B's end and B goes in search of A, but A is nowhere to be found,
    and C and D make off with the trunk

Long are the lazy man's laws, the kittens are in the kitchen, the child's chin aids
    pronunciation

Maybe I'm dreaming I'm naked except for a long black t-shirt I'm dreaming

Bring on the aspirin and bread, the vitamin C and gin

We have fourteen names for blue and that doesn't even count "meridian"

Diderot, Audrey Hepburn, Hegel, Charles Dickens, and Gertrude Stein

Shadow bird shouting

White coral fencing

The butcher on Sunday, Pablo Ruiz, lives south of here (in F____) and has five
    kids—how full of vitality he is

She leaves us behind in the interstices of competence

Origami, irreverence, sand on the wing of an ibis

She drops a bucket down a thick well, she whacks a golfball longer than a marble

Rude and shoed, should and lead, reed

21

A cow goes off and with it three crows in a sycamore tree cawing "awe," "ha-
ha," "off," "ah"
I apologize, dearest one, that was your dream, mine was different
The present king of California is tall, long-lived, and she bounces on her bed
Shocking
Why blame oneself for one's virtues
Two sacks, sails slack, sadness sinks into the inland saga
Ribaldry comes to mind, ten guys descending, pigeons escaping
Tessellated battlements rise, frazzled
Crickets are chirking, the frogs ribbet, the owls howl, and the snakes…what are
they doing
That is what the censor stole
After that duration picks up speed again
Seven fruits are simmering and their jam will be done just in time for the toast
now on the hearth and a bit too close to the flames for comfort
Inconceivably Flagstaff, unlikely Boise, never Garberville
One of two good eagles has taken a cat

22

Here's to the dissident apple—olla

Various insults, prolonged ironies

At the tip of each of his ten fingers Spiderman has a gland and under his arm he
carries an oboe

Off goes a shorthaired old dog and its indented plump brown haunches follow

A winter maple harbors many angles

First the beginning, then the middle, and then the interminable part

We come to a number, 38, its bowl

A missionary pointed to the rat and one cannot say a terrible thing in a better
way than that

Go far over stones, said the rooster to the turtle

It's to the side that the soft fat falls as the old woman lolls, flesh hefted toward
the heart or away from it as she tosses it

Going off with a stopwatch in one hand and a centipede in the other is a
crossing guard named Ned

The very fact of pointing to something commits the person who is pointing to
the conviction that there is something there, to the existence of what
she's pointing at

Daughter precedes dog

Envy invades the piazza, placidity is botched, thinking back will fail

23

It seems like only yesterday that we bribed the police and went north into the mountains
F expresses peremptory rage, P's blood pressure plummets, D reminds us that
        hummingbirds don't swarm
We experience wit, it comes garnished with mint
Shostakovich, baseball (it takes more than stars to make a team), biryani
In the closet hangs a reversible vest, green velvet on the first side, quilted satin on
        the next
The credits roll, white on black
Suddenly the chimp pulled one of them aside, it was a crow
Pumpkin seeds, I have known them from childhood, a French gold coin
The vanishing point is vast
Shouting sledders come over the crest past far-flung sheep
Numbers bear the flash of statistics
One day we pulled up seven stakes and went south by boat to Johannesburg to live a
        sedentary life eating pancakes
It is said that one should rhyme something concave with chaos
Do I know your name, do you know mine

24

A blown single apple drops from a surly bough
Sleep then, X, as we drive out of the mountains
If we'd been armored with understanding, we might have taken up the art of
      scrounging
A wing is a wing of a wingéd for a wingéd is winged with a wing
O experiential friend, let us kiss and make sense
I order / beg / demand that / entreat / require / request / insist that / oblige /
      command / need you: to speak / return / refrain / explain
Sounds known vaguely as "fogs" fringe the songs of the children singing slightly
But wait, the house lacked a laughing room
Here I am, animated to my desk, then box, the context, this jump, the shock
A nasty dog is eating dirty pudding
Vertigo, patches of shadow, the things an anthropologist might know
The downhearted slump like puppets, incapable of speech
Cloud imitated by the sun
It's done quickly and then it stops, it stops something, is that how it measures
      its freedom

25

I'm sick of public life, said the swallow to the bear, said the pigeon in the square
     to a python
O logic, o oaks by the football stadium, o red future rooster
Risotto
The younger child is picking out a tune on a taut rubber band with her teeth
The other person in the waiting room at Big O Tires continues reading *People*
If nothing had a cause, cows could be hatched from robins and balls that fell on
     one day might float on another
Gratefully we watch a silent film
A clown in blue shoes, never slave to imagination, opens a satin-lined traveling
     case and removes a viola
A chill slip of spring's stalled layer comes unfastened
The whispering baker has no bottom to her bowl
O
We must not underestimate the risk of consciousness—it carries us into the
     outer world
The amiable gymnast lunges
There once was a daughter, the second of three—two is good, four is better, she
     said—do you agree

26

Puddings don't have lungs, melons don't have riders
Listen—a female seal, a seaport, and a social world
Come day's end the top of the tree hesitates, pauses, then sweeps on like a
          blackboard eraser to clear the horizon
Sit, Shep, incognito
The lid of the sun is heavy, its lashes blink on the horizon, brushing the curve of
          the sea
So now they want to grant federal coal subsidies
I heard "suspected pipe bomb" as "suspected python"
The first nest empty and deep, at child's eye level, in a young fir tree, of twigs
· Pathos is at the front line of defense against worries as they approach
I remember almost nothing, only that I am in a room with others and we are
          reading through sacks of mail, trying to ferret out spies
She will never believe she's too old to join a band or make quick vertical moves
          on the playing field to really quiet music—she is that still
Then the sparrow went to sleep in a lumber castle
And so we come to chapter LIX, in which I learn that I have failed
Can you believe this shit

27

Everyone stopped

Somewhere unsullied by my thoughts exist pure memories, entirely free of what
I'd make of them, wholly unremembered

If you can write a tragedy you can write a comedy

Perhaps we are the victims of false recognition taken by an acquaintance to be a tree

Vice versa ditto

Sweetness spilling over sour is essential to the sensational flow that characterizes
the continuum we call chocolate

With rapid eye movements I follow the hummingbird over the horse

I don't have much capacity for nonchalance, indifference is a poor substitute

Heel, Fido; fetch, Pal

Time brings whole pieces to the puzzle but not the whole puzzle, the whole picture

It's really her, it's really him

What color is the item that is three-cornered and made of wood

Together with the sun she goes off into the border zone like the middle note of
a chord

Is love the product of judgment

28

Out comes a girl from the quick damnation that brings her forth

I love my eyelids and lips—I, a denizen of the interstitial crack that's home to
dreams that half a hundred hunters have pursued to no avail

Between having to live and having to die, a rabbit has no means of despising the present

The horizon is lidded

She's moving forward, pushing the shopping cart with the tiger that has
temporarily adopted her but isn't hers riding in it, its jaws slightly open, its
tail twitching as it looks back up the street toward the distance from which
they've come

There's resemblance, but it's sweeter, like early carrots

The cow has fallen overboard and it's only thanks to Clara's quick thinking that the
Captain doesn't follow

Next to come onto the market is a kind of panty condom for women to wear

The two are shaking crabs from the bits of raw chicken tied to strings they've
been lowering into the shallow waters of the lagoon and pulling up in the
summer sun back into the lagoon so they can crab some more

I slide the side of the conic end of a Derwent 7B "graphic pencil" across a small
patch of the page, abruptly change its course, giving an angle to the
deepening dimension of a lead cloud

They took everything away—the nose, the mouth, and then the ears

Why not associate small dogs with cold butter, hesitation with play, finger puppets
with habit, ogling with red buttons

Me too

Thinkers get driven past their goal by the sheer momentum of their thinking

29

Ghosts are the shadows of knowledge we crave

My computer's spellchecker resists "thou," it wants "I" to speak to "though"

If you pay too much attention to your feet when jumping from rock to rock you'll…

She tilts the pencil, draws still

There's a small spider overhead and a paper bag of recyclable cans on the floor, a
       black tote bag saying outside of a dog a book is a man's best friend and
       inside a dog it's too dark to read hangs from the knob of the kitchen
       door, beside the toaster the coffee in the yellow cup advertising cheese
       supérieure en poids et qualité is getting cold

Keep telling me

Take as a case in point a duck's noun, going around even now the islands of the separate

As privately—even secretly—as one's response to music, one…and one

Think of all that you see

As a child I used always to read a book lying on my side continuously, head resting
       on palm, and now I read upright repeatedly

To come, to go—around the lake, behind the house, into the city, over the
       bridge—to pass judgment

Strike palm against pail

Monkeys zero in, we're in an "us place"—wide—it's a game ground, without lights

Now for wildlife comedy

30

And the poplars in the wind

It's Monday, and Tuesday is already under way, Wednesday having fled several
      days ago to join yesterday in the immense realm that we'll one day know
      as that of the adjacent-to-the-real

Even the great botanist Carl L thought the fern dust he found hovering close to
      the ground as puzzling as his own nature

She walks awhile unreconciled a hundred miles through chamomile

The play of the imagination is violent

I see a yellow pumpkin on a dozen desert stumps

Is passion a model for patience then: patience the proof, the patch, the put on and
      putting upon

The narrative zigzags but has no name though it's called Assailed and then Curtailed

Chip is the name of a fallen sparrow who listens to some girls as they stack scraps
      of lumber at dusk around her and declare her safe for the night

Waving a pinwheel in my enthusiasm I advance

Along comes a duck waddling by through a flock between the eyes

An serum, an man, an bad job, an bomb and then a other bomb

I first read it eleven days ago but as if unconsciously, that is I...

How can they say that flowers are free natural beauties but horses are not

31

Three barbarians are on the bank of a river whose beauty is theatrical, so they are
 doing blue things, bovine things, emitted things, sand-bottomed things,
 reflective things, things leaving playful impressions
I cannot hear except with eyes
What of the boy, the house—the boy dazzled by house—and what of the unhorsed
 girl, you ask, and I say, the girl is horsed again and the boy has laughed
Along comes a moment—unspent, uninterrupted, arriving incognito
Always add
Then I bought the groceries today from my favorite checker Dave the union
 activist and motorcyclist who's now got his gray hair pulled back in a
 miniscule ponytail
If night were endless and swirled with the sounds of a river whose current carries
 stones, then our travels by bed could be perilous
We begin our investigations in a haunted house of many living creatures which,
 like mementos, carry their own memory charge, lots of energy
Noise and noise shown concurrently in play, hurriedly calling for father
Let's walk under trees with people on grass toward a house invisible to everyone else
You have an egg in your hand and you are putting your toes down ahead of your
 heels, you are breathing on your fingertips, you have an avocado in your
 hand, and against the chill of stupidity you exercise irony
The batted particular ball goes over the wall and there's no reunification and return
And is this why we are so fond of having feelings
Impediments fly

32

Humans are the pulled teeth of Titans

Take Vivaldi, or Willie Nelson

By virtue of a miniscule transition I find myself suddenly on a blue rooftop

The horse is black, its legs long and slender, it sets its feet down precisely, almost
        delicately, on the icy trail, blowing steam from its nostrils

And the sight of migrating birds—how terrifying! no wonder divines read flying
        flocks as presaging disaster

Hoping for insight (but gaining none), I pause to consider a word that surfaced in a
        dream I've just remembered, but I've forgotten the word

Do you think you look like your shadow

Let's play with absolute abandon and thereby intimate the possibility of a very
        different life

Rain falls, with its many syllables—the ultimate authority is the sun

Let's play dominoes, eat artichokes, finger the wind

A head appears over a cloak

Materials of twist are seized and become twisted materials

Dear reader, were you ever a girl

The camel-faced animal flattens back its ears and faces me, appearing to snarl, silently

33

Silently

Bring, buy, catch, seek, teach, and think, unrhyming in the present but
rhyming in the past

I've just gone out for a good laugh at sunset

L is for language, P is for baked alaska

The middle of a sonnet—that which holds its parts and holds them apart—will
be found at its end

Along comes a boy skating on the ice with a 104 degree fever

There's a statue in the little park that I revisit to circle, go back to chastise,
return to admire—it is said to love solitude

Let's bring two things together that don't seem to have anything to do with
each other—a wet windowsill, say, and a white tiger—and see what they
have in common

My eyes have filled

For example, a cormorant cannot—and *should not*—be said to have any point at all

That's a bushel of wheat; that's a secretary; that's a night flight to Bangkok—
but which *one*

I don't much like epigraphs: they tend to offer false promises in the guise of
false conclusions

Very slowly with my eyes I follow the lines between boards that link the
bedroom floor to the equator

53 degrees Fahrenheit near dark at midnight, the curtains hanging still, no
birdsongs, nothing defies gravity, only occasional street sounds break up
the lack of experience, the failed attempt, the infinity of possible degrees
at whose center stands the imaginary pole toward which the dipper dips

34

It will take two days of steady rowing to take us to where we're going

She says nothing, sees nothing, pinching folds into the blanket, pleating the sheet, hour by hour

Creation myths are always tales of cruelty, in which forms are forced out of ambiguous material's amorphous lumps, chunks, splotches, blobs

Along comes a mounted rifleman, advancing from memory to consciousness or from dream to waking life or from imagination to censure

The solitude of the country hotel has tempted me and in response I want to compose a couplet for the guest book

A magic encyclopedia, a marshmallow afloat on hot chocolate, a man with money in his hat

Two boys and two girls, working together, have successfully recaptured a maverick month-old calf and we praise them for their heroism, such heroism is never accomplished by halves

The people leaning out their windows may just be spitting or watching an arrest

It began with an apple and ended with an opera influenced by jazz

Walt Disney and Alfred Hitchcock: two caricaturists of the mid-twentieth century American psyche

Leaves lie afloat in the cold quiet water that's just now supporting a damselfly

Dazzling as a flower head, noteworthy as a crocodile in Paris, the intelligencer— readily, rapidly, auspiciously, unofficially—cavorts under overcast skies

The eyes are like half-open mouths that visibility causes to stutter

There will never be an adequate explanation for how or why it happened

35

The Eye of the Storm

There are many weathers, some that shrink as the day goes by, some predatory,
        some like feathers randomly falling on distant interesting lands
The young win a game against far older rivals and people step out of shops,
        houses, apartment buildings, banks—they converge on the sidewalks
        and overflow onto the street, just becoming aware of the rioting that's
        about to break out: two excitements
Along come the tall young woman with the small yellow dog and her "come
        on, follow me" with the darker other woman in a red coat with her
        "different materials are differently affected by the sun" and the man
        with the cell phone in a pouch hooked on his belt, along comes the child
        with her "that's so cool" and camera
And the dead?—they eat peas and dandelions from the roots up, they eat the
        roots of daffodils, redwoods, and roses
Our investigation now stumbles on and fearfully, clumsily, entirely, we follow,
        groping, greeting, grinding
There once was a young woman who late in life grew a second, small,
        superfluous tongue under the first, but she could find no purpose for it
        and from lack of use it soon withered away
The chair is red—the red of a pudding, a camel, and a cartoon
One in daisy white, the other in dairy white—twice the same girl with black
        shoes in two different dresses and a girl in mushroom white
The silent ceramic poet glazed by rising fire roars "Love" and at that inevitable
        note of hopelessness the silent ceramic cracks
I will be cruel, said Cruelty, but that is a given, said the girl with a grin who
        was not *a* girl but *the* girl, ferocious and uncruel
But let us celebrate what was as that which is and the very very slow violence of
        forests, the gentle violence of the trees
Let us take our surrogate selves out and leave them like guinea pigs to sniff and
        browse on swirls while we sit cross-legged in a sun-swept amphitheater
O child, be contemporary, your soul an ornament of consciousness
In the statue's rock is insouciant life, respite, lingering, hard

For Susan Bee
In memory of Emma Bee Bernstein

36

The pansies look and watch and see, and the daisies radiate, and the field
    billows, and a robin rummages, and the sound of the unmasked
    demolition of a bridge travels upriver but no farther than the waterfall
    that drowns it out, my prison
A young woman named Sal can stand on her own shapely feet, that's the idea,
    banging on boxes, putting knobs to the ground, shouting "heads up" so
    the ceiling is visible
O yes
I've been tied to a rail
Knock, knock
The smallest unit of time is "from here to that star"—it's a *light trip*
All prancing proud horses sweat milk and are mothered by low-lying clouds
Mother, Mother, I got married and I kept God entirely out of the game
What is the name of this flower
In a collection of aphorisms the aphorisms dance, clumsily stomping on each
    other, tripping each other up, trying to outlast each other
Tooth and palm, mandible and parasol—when the queen is gone, the workers
    become fertile
It is from love that the concept of "intervening days" arose, and the notion of
    "the future" came from love too, but it is death that gave us "history"
The cilia shiver, the flagella wiggle—the cilia whistle
Girls, my anchor has run out of print—what is my scientific name

37

Any thought of arousal here would be deeply inappropriate—any thought would be
Ribaldry, eloquence
There is a face hand-painted on the window-shade clinging to a fraying rope forty
      feet above the street
An image flickers, then another, and another, and another, and there's the sting of
      it, the picture
We can't stop life from bellowing at death and life has the advantage since death
      can't bellow
There were not enough faces in the mirror for her selves
Innumerably unlocked and cobalt-candied and sun-candied, a kitchen counter
      hangs in the sun under the sky
Daily the dead do up in us
She is as silent and solemn as the sun overcome by fun
A tiny pool of dark rain water shimmers in the empty sockets of the statue's eyes
Welcome the new medieval concentric
A long story of adventure falls into a time frame
We will depart from the individual quarantine, exit the squeezed altitude
The most insectoid thing I can think to utter is et cetera

38

According to one theory of the novel, narration is a man's piano at which a woman sits
We will elegize and elegate and make loud elegies on the demise of public education
The bird is writ tide wild
I cannot be joking, nor providing examples
The wild stars are always around receding daily from ideas
We are in a spiritual shackle—we promise
The children refer to the bed as "The Kennel" and to sleep as "Something like Mars"
This is the hard English of shit, shack, slam
As a child, on a bed, at the starting gate, even today—imagine it
When we have loved, we have pressed cause to cause
Solidarity, particularity
Storage disappears, legislation appears
All of the wow come and would be if could be
I spotted a shoplifter, a teenaged girl, and turned immediately away so as not to see
    so as to preserve her innocence, at least for me

39

You hike in your chair, you swim in your bed, you speed up the Volga in a boot
This is not in the language of the hour of eclipse of an onion of holes
O thorns of the black bougainvillea, fronds of the purple palm, you have thrust
       your shadows into the garden of my friend
I saw a whole field of battle on a pole, in a peapod, at the bottom of a graveyard pit
Rasputin had voltage, Pushkin had swords, and history is a suitcase filled with
       money—to unlock it you need a stiff dead fish
There were once small men as clever as mice, as cruel as ice, and they ruled over
       numbers on the faces of clocks
"Voyage in place: that is the name of all intensities"
Cat's code at gift's edge
An old year falls off a horse backward into a cart—such is the name of one
       unlocked constellation
A whole backdrop disappears to a silenced body
The logic of metaphor passes through a zero and points invisibly over an edge
In the resonant room around a chlorinated pool a mesmerist cures agricultural drunks
It will take much more than a mighty hedge to stop a wren
How brave a sun is that

In memory of Alexei Parshchikov

40

Thoughtsound, background

For the painter had grown wild, and the dead girl: how murdered

Let's sleep out on the porch on this moonless night and barely glimpse the Pleiades

Music of delicate arrivals, pluralities predicted in a statistician's handbook

Living an unstraight chain, she..., or I..., and we..., they..., then she, he..., she,
   you, ... but she

We utilize the valorizing conditioner, the volumizing shampoo, the volatizing mousse

There once was a woman with assurance and wit who considered all isms counterfeit

Portage, township, cartilage, wiggle-room

The male turkey with the raging battle wattle and gaping mouth whose outspread
   sprawling tail feathers he turns to us we name Bad Beggar and his every
   expression is an angry supplication

And she's never willful because she ever won't but was and is

The saint in question, the baroque saint fiddling in the heraldic painting, is
   ungovernable life itself

Scrambled is the logosphere, perpetuous is the contrasphere

I am a rhino and the grass is gray, the prairie undulates as if there were only a
   single mind to which one goes for one's thoughts

Is that ever irreverent

41

The spoons have clattered
Aren't children little pears and observant birds
I note that the green blanket is askew again briefly
I have flung my sweater over the banister again
The corn cockle is buoyant
There was of course the matter of the curious descent into a mine and the
        terrible ascent of children out of context hauling ore
Brevity is not child's play
Today a man in a green leather hat advised me to sink my shovel
If I were to write a letter to a one-time friend now she might not remember who
        I was which in any case is not who I continue to be
Tchaikovsky died when he was fifty-three
Believe me
Long ago I was once in Seville in a blue dress that could be washed and dried in
        ten minutes
The tales I used to tell myself no longer do
None of this is true

42

Oppidan, urbanite, bumpkin blowing dragonflies—they stop at scathing dahlias in
        the full moon stoppage of a horizontal day
It can't not be day *and* night backing the quotidian extraordinary real time shape
The seriocomic quiet mite goes from wayside weed to woman and back to weed again
Yikes
There can't be any difference, so there can't be barriers
The detective-ghost is bound to a canoe just approaching a waterfall
Crow petals, stubborn pinging wind, croaking frogs casting meadow beads
Naked walkers between eyes hike downhill, moving on through blue-black green
Jubilant white half-orphaned voyeur bounding gladiola dog dawdles without dwindling
The stand is outlasting, the horizon outraces the setting
New words, new habitations—walking mind is sonic bliss (zoning, but not out—
        we can't argue about that now)
Long from then as indistinct from now as woman from animal-dayfly the runner
        did, will, does, won't, happened to, can't help but fling gladdening buds at
        the slower buttercup floor boards
Only hearing, taking no other action, one deracinates
Are the four or eight or myriad sides of living vertical? horizontal? parallel? strewn

For Leslie Scalapino, in memory of abiding friendship,
strong argument, and the love that was the sound,
shape, and substance of her thought

43

Burrs of blue forget-me-nots borne on bold-fingered whole strokes hang on the
      wall of the room to which they stick
The man with a rake on the beach did assist
Ghosthood, floating head
It wasn't curiosity that killed the man who wore no hat that bore no band that
      had no stripes that were a subdued shade of gray
Have you ever seen a donkey go this way and that way
The nights are large increments of life
It is sometimes in the subtlety of the ordinary that you are relieved of the
      necessity of answering
O handwritten fan of the husky chanteuse, o purveyor of bulbs of blue impasto,
      o patter of the pocket of the chevalier, o lost hemisphere
There—out of the cowled shell a father turtle's head turns
The wide gate swings to the consequences of use
Two or three bears—more or less (who's counting?)—that had more or less
      terrorized what is variously known as "the area" or their "home
      territory" or "the neighborhood" or "the locale"—have been
      "relocated"—more or less
The tree in the ivy extraordinarily looming is of a kind that palms the light as
      the sprinklers turn
Take forty winks and forty more
Language is as blind as sleep

In memory of my father

44

O mighty survivors who outlive your outlife, we see you
Self-adhesive, art cohesive—follow the end-words to some conclusion
Beaky indent, avian daydream, crested mustang in the wind, and a meadow mushroom
Every doctor pleads and prognosticates and pees, male or female
She does not, will not, should not, did not, can not, would not, separate,
      compartmentalize, segment, subdivide, parcel out, and does, shall, did, can,
      will, must pool, plummet, plumb, and plot
The witch of the micro-wilderness between minutes lifts her fist and counterpunches
This is about glue, so I will google glue, then google google glue
Whoever you are now, you are folding the laundry, your name begins with an X or
      Q or G and you pay no attention to he, or she, or me
Such an effort it takes to go on a roll
Largeness, talc, a compendium of opinions that change with changing
      circumstances, and a fourth thing (perhaps a deposit slip)
I look at a page covered with words and all I see is bugs and that makes me neither
      original, imaginative, nor smart in my opinion
You were born like a rocket and live with fins
I'm working small
More language

45

If a woman were to rhyme *district* with *compact* would she have time, would she
      follow her daughters
The blue is sky all day
It was 6:43 pm when I wrote that it was 6:39 pm—that is time for you
The barred walled, the barred wailed
The little group around the bed engage in a flurry of word play, meanings are
      bent, words are pressed by etymology, it's all amorous activity
Hard-won banality—it's the basis for the pioneer's ultimate success
Let's amble between the seedling trees to the bull ring to watch young picadors
      on bicycles taunt a rubber toro
Repetitions, situations, and types—these are dandelions, those are stripes
The resonant round world on which the children stomped was a vast fat
      declarative drum
Chance is old hat, fates abound
Lights out, narcissi, it's time for a capacious farewell
Are those girls gigglers
I was thrown so far by the bucking horse that I fell outside the circle time
      travels, said a blue angel made of pebbles
We are wanting, we are waiting, we are warning

46

A dream is a poor location for memories of things one hasn't noticed, things
    scarcely worth noticing
Whew—my head is like a chrysanthemum held upright on my neck
Underwriting the stick figure with its stock-still demeanor is its caption: "A
    Minute Goes By"
Figs on a spot
In due course anti-lions and anti-asps will befriend wandering humans on sailing
    ships propelled by calm
Enter two guinea pigs, one black and one white, gender of each only to be imagined
It's impossible to discontinue
Once there were four children and their great-grandmother was the duchess of a
    distant island known for its berries, sail-makers, sullen lice, bears, and a
    dark shepherd whose name was Daisy
How very like pickles the leaves on the beautiful branches hang in the rain
"Today is today is today yet again"
I cannot play the instrument of lamentation, it's impossible to tune
History comes upon a clutch of dog's eggs in a ditch that's plastered over and
    painted green as the grass whose insects sting
I have not left yet, she says—I have not yet made that distinction
All dusty begonias continue to frolic

47

Alice faces and Agatha faces and Bob faces and Ben faces and Didier faces and bone
       flat faces and collie faces and still spider faces
Science produces its nineteenth explanation: the world has separated from the sun
Polka walkers waltz through the watercress, blonde-billed ducks build opulent nests
Literature is catapulted into reality by desire—writing is literature failing to hear
Hey hey, ho ho, baby with a diaper on can always go
It's late—evidently, theoretically, hypothetically, by all accounts, or so they say
There was hot weather in late August, rising all day from the night, and I watched
          the ants on the sidewalk impossible to stop—interference simply spurring
          them on with the tune in my head, thematic, like crunching on corn,
          afraid of the sudden movements of planes, gravity and heat creating an
          equilibrium which kept everything in motion but prevented it from going
          anywhere—and I waited with the special character of relaxed interest
          that one feels when reading a newspaper, every item independent of every
          other and of you, the war not yours, the money not yours, the execution
          not yours, the entire month a prolongation not yours, a referral not to
          you, it can't be—the sun vamping, the sun tangled on the lake, late, the
          lines wobbling, evangelists coming to the door and achieving nothing, the
          moment gone
One can't blame the broken window on the rock, when in truth it is fate that's to blame
Along comes someone down the street ranting about some "world parrot" and
          raising her arms as if raising arms to aim and shoot so realistically that she
          is spun completely around by the imaginary rifle's imaginary recoil and she
          staggers out of view
My old grandma took me to the Moulin Rouge where they offered glasses of gin for
          nickels and everyone raised a toast impartially, first to the government, then
          to anarchy
It isn't time that takes each new night away and returns the old day and puts a
          period to our desires
It rains and the empiricist drinks from an upturned cabbage leaf
There's not much to be seen out the window at the moment, just a dog, a soup
          spoon, the dull eyes of a damaged statue
At the moment, chance is as obligatory as tradition once was

48

How do you do, Froth Lavender, says the goldfish to the cappuccino—it is with just
        such conversational overtures that the cup of human consciousness overflows
Draw the eyelids over the eyes, close the quilt over the ears
The sunlight has lit silver quivers on the rosemary—it has so many aromatic fates
Tired workers trudge on rubber, hats off, losing boots, as they enter the vestibule
        which will appear, though as an afterthought, just inside the door of the shop
A non-sequitur is a song of experience
Don't give me a rose—I prefer the inner peace of nasturtiums from which unsung
        earwigs crawl
See men, and anxieties of, danger of, expected earnings of, lifespan of Rauritanian,
        musicianship of, soldiers as, suicides of, women imitators of
Rarely ridiculously although idiosyncratically loosely, the parent mediates a dispute
Crow is mocking cow, duck is mocking truck, trowel is mocking soil, and soil's worm
        is mocking mockery while we watch the clock clocking mockery's intervals
He or she who makes a bed may not be a carpenter despite the nails driven deep into
        the head
Just then the first—the very first—drop of rain hits the sidewalk
An allegory is an index of inexperience
Give me an odious word
A soul came to me, an excited infantile voyeur—he was cute until he began to crawl,
        always scuttling toward the future while getting history ass-backwards

49

A star screen shimmers under the moon over the urban center flashing on it red
    and green
I'll have a suspension, mustard, topicality, glue
Kitty, kitty, kitty, kitty
Whipped gouache just about covers the situation
In the Musée Unless there's a fallen nest on display empty of an egg once
    belonging to a song bird, species unknown, which had sung
See *style*, see *working late*, see *mismatched socks*, see *polyphony*
It is the fate of logic infinitely to undo closure but that's just to say that it's the
    fate of logic infinitely to be logical
So like a man goes into a shop and there's like this other man in there whom he
    thinks he recognizes and he says like do I know you
The fallen grass in winter sprawls its spring
Regulations state that the pier can accommodate no more than one troupe of
    acrobats, thirty fishermen, or fifty tourists
Yo
The child never gives up her secret, which—don't tell—is that she has a secret,
    and her secret has a penis
We will lose another day from the inner picture—days are not ineradicable there
What is it that one is autobiographical about

50

And after the river of your inlet withdraws, sound, sing to ground
Having fun, funsters, I ask
When a point is cut, call it puller, pint, and put
The world is your mind's bucket
Once it was enough to be melodious, when every song was like a nail in the jaw
As I do now
On day one the friendly girl rides a pony, on day two she wears the number 14
      and drives a ball
It's like would will I when then won't it
Take the word upholstery—it refers, perhaps, to the hard bosom of an unbridled
      horse fleeing a yellow lion
You have climbed a fifty-foot fir and the sap has grown dirty on your knees
There is no ism that will suffice
And now for a little drama, a startling performativito: I present the children,
      who are aromatic and unquantifiable, they thunderclap, antecede,
      honeybee, and bicycle
Whatever it is, it is not a capybara because they are a smaller, piglike animal
What are the words for points of distant time that spread unevenly

51

Afloat in a glass-bottom boat, I see into the sea—a miniscule emerald memento

That the strongest social bonds are forged by language doesn't nullify the power
that dancing around the puppet effigies of the men in power has

On the solemn face of the glinting belly is a button baby

You have to know how to roll on the horizon

Followers follow, possibles possibulate, coruscations consider, blood coagulates

An allegory is a depiction of something that can't be depicted

Mathias Madrid thrusts his fist toward his face in a mirror, Millicent Malcolm
pets a faithful falcon on a perch, Margaret Mason makes fig jam to serve
on cold toast with hard cheese

The pyrotechnical expanse, lacking azure, makes do with blatant blackness,
unspoken light

Winter's cover's curled back by adjectives—whacking winter's roadside cover

Stained owls and up over the ill rabbits they fly

Several hours go by but hours are impossible to perceive

I market, am marketed, mark, remark

We walk down a street under windows that let in noise that might prompt
someone asleep in the room to dream of drummers, flautists, a man on
stilts with a tuba, a sextet of wise-cracking girls, a band of baritone boys

What is it ghosts wonder

52

The situation calls for a rhyme: gelatin with skeleton
Each wave carries its own paint, sweet pink or rancid chartreuse
End here, fait accompli
The old white woman in the long black skirt pauses at the kitchen sink, struck by
      sudden consciousness
Between frames monsters replicate—each one unattributable
When one glimpses beauty and looks away, then spaces, bare-throated, are feminized
How are mountains like rucksacks or blankets drawn up to a dreamer's chin
We live on a world from which metamorphoses are drawn
Nearest you stands a porous rose among dull begonias, snow shakes on seashells
      under on oncoming train
Some things are like plastic and will last forever, which is long after we have
      stopped singing of experience
Shall I compare the apple's stem to an umbilical cord or a puppy's tail
The invisible issues an invitation cursed with infinite complications
Air now fills the area
More rare than abnormality, more spare than grand formality, is plastic triviality

53

Out of cardboard, out of bounds, out of marmalade, a biplane ascends, out of
    sight, out of it
Peanut sauce, tofu, and grains of boiled rice fly from the mouth
With the sweetness of solicitude, with a glower, with a shout forgotten by the
    moon, the room is full
Look to the right: things just as they are
The ocean hides the reaching octopus in her long and devious courses
I did nothing whatsoever, my emotions were normal, and I wasn't cold
Nature offers allegorical images—clouds awaiting captions, mountains hiding
    minerals that are better termed mysteries
There was a small woman who never went out so as all the better to care for her
    house, and there was a bald culprit who lived in a tower all the better to
    spy on his spouse, for which reasons, among many others, the woman and
    the culprit never met
Let's now proceed, go, venture forth, carry on, continue, undertake, set out, walk off
You say experience is virtual when you say nothing at all
1, 7, 10, 16, 19, 27, 31, 40, 43, 55, 65, 70, and counting
I thought I saw a female—or perhaps transsexual—peanut, I thought I saw an
    amber—or perhaps ambiguous—horse
At a picnic, succinctly, so as to downplay/minimize/desentimentalize/neutralize
    and make no claim to its purport, I referred to the death of the mother
    of the child-at-my-side—but already, entering/saying/writing/recording
    that here, I've committed a betrayal
Is it too late to watch another episode

54

I make this translation myself, and if there are parts that should be renounced,
tell me now and I'll renounce them

An ink man on paper, a chalk man on a sidewalk, and a shadow man, a sleeping
man, an ash man, a man of bones—well, they don't scare me

Take a look

Can it be that you will never in English, in French, Swahili, Urdu, or Spanish be
together again—bare-butted, neck to neck, stark-naked

The untimely appearance of a cloud directly overhead and completely visible
between buildings (it looks like an Airedale standing on a ball) casts no
more than a passing shadow

Brillat-Savarin says that "anyone who can pile up a great deal of money easily is
almost forced, willy-nilly, to be a gourmand"

What have we there if not a haiku in a cart

Over and over I replay the argument, suffer differently or at different points,
make a few alterations

We are asked to blacken A's nose and dot her cheeks to mark the pores from
which the cat's whiskers will grow

A brain has a stomach, lungs have hands, people everywhere slip away, leaving
others behind, some ironic, some lazy, some militant

The preparations precede the project and then we plunge

In front of the windows an austere garden murmurs in a shell

We've a sauce of chopped red onion and mint in balsamic vinegar for the salmon
now poaching in white wine and water

The gay sea unlocks and calls her random stars

55

The son jumps in, tapping the sides of a silver triangle that rings a sturdy inner silence
"As for memory, it…is much closer to knowledge than to life"
The sky is two years wider
Coherent reorganization of contents: shifting, providing, measuring, marking
They have beliefs so primitive and strange of some supreme consciousness of them
       that the humans are more foolish than hens
Toe to cobblestone, linen to shoulder, and one out of order
If vacillation of mind is to continue, we must skate deeper, upholding delighted skulls
Air to be tugged, air untranslated
Her name was C but we called her L and Ponder and could not caption her and wonder
Small begonias are easily bruised in the melancholy of habituation
We have no alternatives but alternatives, so let's alternate
One last caveat
Time doesn't fly—therefore I cannot have saved the flamingo
Words are never with life more clever than the life itself that comes over the
       mountains separating the eastern sea from the western city with daughters

56

It should not be strange to be a woman rewarded

Letters click as they wander, shift as they ascend, their altitudes attain autobiography

Next you are like dry steps' passing sound and fall, and then you are like
          sweetened grapefruit

Everything applies in the hyper-patterning that retrospect attempts and to which
          the irreverent response is "How splay"

In the small houses of the children in the house there are always complex
          simplicities and one was a vast pink stuffed equine thing called Star

Wet Brahms

Revocation of harm

By moving from window to window and carefully recording at each what we see, we…

It is time you were told of the time I failed to defend the bull and indeed rejoiced
          in its murder

This is *not* hypocritical

The statue at its fullest is emptiest of meaning

She speaks to another not about sex but about a particular game of truth

Sonorousness facilitates the descent of sunny motes from the ponderosa

These dancers have fleas—or, shall we say that fleas live on the planet of these dancers

57

Useless lighthouse, and the bucket on the beach, the tattered begonias
Forget examples—there's not an entity or detail around that isn't more than a
　　　　mere example
What's truly funny
Once upon a time there was a mouse, and there was a cactus and a pair of very small
　　　　rubber boots with a hole in the sole of the left one, and now that I think
　　　　back I remember that there was a baby on a barge in a lake full of flowers,
　　　　and out of these there's a story to weave and probably more than one
The music changes at the mantel, the bassoonist is baffled, the synchronizer fails
Rickety marble, wet wood, the road narrowing into the distance and then
　　　　turning around a rock
Is it empty good writing, is it research, resurgence, repartee
8, 9, 10, 11, minus 31, 8
A stranger creates an occasion
Lewd silver sea, your bigness carries barges as noon stands in grass
See, I got cops—or they got me; so says the melancholy memoirist from the
　　　　anarchy of her dreams
Clear is the sojourn
In the stiff air, down the unbalanced wind, over dusty culverts, women bear
　　　　their hot cells of benevolence
Are all wonders small

58

A star passes to a neighboring star a no longer extant nation one Monday night
        over Via Francisco Sosa, but through which window

She as she, splendid as sand spun into glass

That was only that then thinly

In the middle of myself is a strange sound from a wideness of wires

The other merely wonders, "Why is that person glancing at me"

We are cheering for *both* teams

The sky is a deep tray, the stars are oats, the earth is divided into nations, the
        great-winged albatrosses remain at sea

Confidence goes much against each introspective individual but likes great walls
        and bold frescoes

The residents called the police and the police said why didn't you discourage
        development of the park lands in the first place and the residents said we
        want to live someplace safe, sanitary, and decent and the police said if
        you want new art you'll have to maintain your old buildings

And there bright as a warbler is a wedge of spangled cantaloupe on a fork
        moving in the sunlight

A song to pass along, saying something, forms

It has been said that modernity has an abiding interest in moving along both roads,
        the road to no particular purpose and the road to power and acquisition

There must be something other than a temporal method for being what we are

I'm like a clam, a clam with two hands, a two-handed clam I am, bam bam

59

Sir

That March morning spotlight fell, felt, can't field, can't follow

Smaller as some days get, they may be inextricable from the bigger ones

I haven't written the faintest idea

A cut of day, a caught night—we don't need new motives for loving

It is early morning in the late Cretaceous

Sitting just under the swimming west that remains afloat on worthy objects,
we... or they...or she...or you... or I, alone...

I have true independence of memory

It is as a natural Darwin that the bold painter saturates her curiosity with color
where a skeptical world would see only earthworms and mud

Are we not the sticky future

The lights behave negatively and are sent home

It is good to wear shoes stronger than sneakers for crossing and recrossing and
never getting across the necropolitan dunes

One can begin to remember from anywhere, anything can get remembering
going, something can get one doubting, nothing is perfectly flat, and
everything is hidden

Here is porcelain for incredulity, milk for irony, a broom for irreverence, a
harpsichord for banter and lack of necessity

60

The pine branches reach—see the rain, the sun, the edge of the moving air,
    three goats

Girls on razor scooters turn the corner and scoot

Autonomy actually shows, it shines amidst the stars of decision

I sacrifice hearing to writing, I return to the back of the train

Surrounded by nothing but tattered island nasturtia, the shoveler is prepared to
    exclaim, "Grief exterior, grief prison"

Beastly pine cones are falling from the sky

Down in the middle, and a soft wall, the midnight breeze billows

Check the role, the rock, the rule

From cardboard pressed to ginger, water spilled on a list, salt sprinkled over...

Why so many references to dogs, purple, and bananas

Then the carnival—it came up afterwards like a vermillion buttress to say of
    itself "it appears"

Wren in a ragged bee line, flora sleeping live

Yuki, Felicia, and Maxwell have between them $13.75, and they are hungry as
    they enter the small café, where they see a display of pies and decide to
    spend all their money on pie there and then—how much pie will each
    get to eat if each pie costs $5.25

Invincible is my myopia, great is my waist, choral are my ideas, wingéd are my
    eyebrows, deep is my obscurity—who am I

61

I want to find the thing, I want it to accumulate, rotate, and not culminate
The egg is milk at rest and an orb under asymmetrical conditions
Perhaps judgment is only for the mind, perhaps the key word is juggler, perhaps
    space is effaced in a mirror
A wry smile sets a horizon
Now everything is ready
I'm not bored, it's more like I'm in a daze, uneasy, but not ill-at-ease, I'm not
    thinking about myself, I'm not thinking about anything, I'm just
    staring into space, pausing, waiting, with a slight sense of approaching
    disappointment
And fake and successful and posthumous and giving me a hand in the kitchen
She hunts from turning ears
I once knew a man who kept a small orchestra in a suitcase, and I once knew a
    woman who kept to herself
And with that the kitchen timer rang and I ran to attend to the split pea soup
    in the pot
A cool scroll of antelopes, trapped, not *by* but *in* humans
O museum, O masochism, O mammary glands
I am whitewashed under the name of anarchy, protest, community
Have they not great American tusks, have they not African citizenship

62

Into the disordered shortening of a circle comes this little fury, this abdicated
        panic, this dirty Venus, this resemblance to nothing we know of the dead
Sky simultaneous bud, cavity contemporaneous slight
And from the tree a ripe peach falls and a puff of dust rises, gently circles, drifts,
        spreads, holds its shape, dissipates, and settles under the tree again and
        on the weeds nearby
Once there was a woman I'll name another day and in her care were eight
        well-matched strong pelicans who flew low over the sea in careful
        configurations that brought her aesthetic pleasure and more fish than
        she or they could eat
Life is rife with erasure and time is rich with delay
Immediately the eater spots some defects (bits of meat, scraps of green)
No, I did *not* forget the sad vagrant shuffling about in his red speckled secrecy
        and I will *never* do so *again*
You've been boasting of your cantaloupe pottage, you've provided us with thin
        toast, your glory increases all about you
Hush—ssshh—what is it
The ancestor wandered toward the horizon, he craved recognition, but eons
        went by and he landed in a circus, there being no other work for a man
        from the gloom of origins
Cousins are composite, constructed, compared
Quick, lively, assembled ripples monitor, mosquitoes spill, and the children
        dine on candy
The sky is another point, this time of ambiguous blue
Why didn't I think of that

63

To be a hill a hill is filled

Let's sing a long song without words: "la dee ah" (ascending) and "ah ew" (warbling) and "diddle diddle dum" (comically) and "hwoo-ohhh" (in a minor key)

The critic has to stay close to her object of interest but she's also got to confess her anxiety, her uncertainty, her criminality

Have I not nematodes in my gut, have I not delusions in my brain, have I not white blood in my veins

Then the rocks—a perfect mirror

I must make my escape, said the sun

Into the jam jars go the peeled and pitted fruits of the sweetening-gatherer's day, into the air go the signs of weightless autumnal decay

The present can't dislodge history, but it is giving us something new to argue about

Friendships are extrinsic to the call to action the moment requires

I have been reliving late at night somewhere in grass or a forest

Daylight and pins, she announces; sandwiches and obligations, geometry and macaws

There was a person harmed, says the Argentinean wife

I have an orange cat who is a jaunty predator, he's bargained with the garden birds and never been a traitor

The void stays forever weightless

64

Thing now tone, aquatic tilt is real, stick and money thieve, turn the future,
      scratch gas, cricket

Listen

Little spider darting out from a hiding place behind a rolodex and racing to a
      cranny between piles of papers: something we saw, wanting it to come
      back, or wanting it to go, like a king when royalty is outmoded

Glenn Gould is still humming along like a Volkswagen on an autobahn

One day a mournful young man spat on a traffic cop's shoe, but the man's name
      was Ferdinando and the cop's name was Matilda, and they lived together
      happily ever after

Actually, I am not addressing myself here to metaphysicians, nor to spirits, nor
      to pedants, because none of these know how to see the particular beauty
      of a rain-soaked field

I believe I have acceded with docility to aesthetic laws—so says Odilon Redon,
      but to what in the world around us might those laws pertain

All good children envy mint, so tune your instruments accordingly, because
      mint is as obstinate as a god

A celebration takes place and in surprise my error is corrected

Parsimonious ethnicity, cowardly mind, constraining gender, uninherited class,
      deracinated citizenship

You are so tired and I am so timing and he is so tidy and then there are those
      others, all so tithed and tipped-off and titanic

Help, I'm clinging to the side of a cliff, gripping a crumpling outcropping of
      rock, a train is rumbling through the valley below, a passenger looks up

Then two tiny birds darted (jetted? bulleted? sped!) from one tree to another
      and I could see a band or spot of yellow on each, but they were too little
      and too fast for me and who cares about identification

I am very busy, I have a lot of energy, I've got a lot of projects underway, I've a
      number of plans, I'm very active, I'm industrious, productive

65

Cat in the redwood, chasing pie

Now in a sequence is a consequence, right

Fred laughs, Ferdie scowls, Felicia strums her thumb, but, as Martha points out,
nothing necessarily follows

You have only to slide some sprigs of thyme after the shallot and lemon into the cavity

In the tale the dachshund wears boots and the little girl, its companion, has a
purse that replenishes itself with money whenever she buys crayons,
cookies, or fruit

War warrant plate daring too doesn't sum it

An autobiography offers a gloss to a life, but it's a translator's gloss, full of
misunderstandings

She dared to ask and get canny and deride servility and temper glass and scatter
candies, and that was a mighty horsewoman indeed, and she rode with
chocolate spurs

I wouldn't say particles exactly, I couldn't capture particles of any single lifetime,
because there is no single lifetime nor solid anchor nor sweaty pathos that
doesn't end up at the bottom of some sea

Slowly she swiftly turns and all that was said is to be long considered

The present cannot decipher

Make it language then, with no pictures

The ponderous sun hangs as rose and cream white fruits must if student loans
doom college graduates to poverty

A love scout, that's the term, is he or she who sometimes finds mourners,
sometimes celebrants, sometimes children, sometimes no one at all

66

Suppose ungainly twigs, somewhat

Lished itivity tent ample crates

You disappear into a duration, the where and while of which is called
Heedlessness, Indifference, Absence, Mischief

Yesterday, let's go out; tomorrow, we were kept indoors, now let's eat grapes

Suppose the poet speaks and the language doesn't answer

The passion has its turf but, whoops—I thought it was better managed than *that*

Nobody moves in the photograph, nor will they ever move

Rally roll and then the little girl went up the tree

Into an L-shaped alley the young son strolls harboring a month's provisions in his
velvet portmanteau

The radiator knocks, the jump rope knots

Digestion proceeds as we sleep, and it is for this reason that we fart upon waking

It had been raining for three days in that interstitial environment, home to local fauns,
where men come out of oaks dark, smart, and with a hint of criminality

Speculate for me

One a tree, softly, two a right eye, tenderly, three a threshold, kindly, four a
mallard, fortuitously

67

Isn't worry wooden

Appearances burn to perfection, the same old frolic, permanent atoms becoming
astronauts and then unbecoming them again

There was never and will be never and once she was like a gazelle commanding a field

Violent is the violin, deep is the speed with which the Great Wall of China
wanders, serene is the soot far up the chimney venting the smoke from
the longlife log

The sun keeps its secret, the daily news is sunk in light

This is a melody played on a cock harmonica, lyrics lost in a story buried under a
bellicose rock

Could she and why

What butter

The barefoot musician fiddles on the ice with greater weight over the years and
the juggler's jugs get lighter

It's not from an aphorism that you'd want our memories to rise—you'd resist,
persist, preside

Life is full of indubitable data, indelicate stuff

Though drawn to the claims of the sky, I duck my vertigo and devour a huge
sandwich, my commitment to gravity, which holds my shadow to the ground

We are subject to the ultimate disorientation, a cloud of invisible power

The sun is sure-fire

68

Before you are set an apple, a gold coin, and a book

So there we were with raptors on a string and you said "your daughter is a
hypocrite" and I said "pleasantries won't make you free"

Is this the appropriate point for me to introduce the story of the floating head
chopped from a sitting boy

I smile full force against a horsefly riot cop

And then: grettable inces, nately posing, mediacy thermore, most mulation—
it's all avid design

Daily life draws us into an endless dialogue and if you ask what the conversation
is about it's about pea pods and labor and allergies and lunch meat and
contraceptive devices ancient and modern

Where rest the increments of a human being's life that's not now soot in a circle

Our memories are made of skinny apples as we tickle nightingales, or of
mishaps for which we blame ourselves so as to gain some distance, or of
balletic burrs carried away on the red paws of a dog described in a book

Don't ask

Past tense, present tense, three legs in a single brown shoe—these are the tale's
principal elements, with innumerable variations possible along the way

We've got to crystal heart hustle, I'm feeling fleeting bug emotions

O milk, o propitiation

It seems to me that we could loop the emphasis and go around and around—*and*
go around and around, and *go* around and around, and go *around* and
around, and go around *and* around, and go around and *around*

Beyond the fence, standing under a tree, the two horses turn to watch me, turn
to watch me, turn to watch me, turn to watch me

69

Eternity goes on for such a long time that nothing can happen to disrupt it

Laughter is encrypted grief, but grief is encrypted laughter, too

Hardly noticed, another apple falls into the yellow grass—an event that changes
the apple, the tree, the orchard, the grass

What's the first thing that comes to mind when someone says the word
"traveler": gypsy? nomad? salesman or saleswoman? tourist? conference-
goer? refugee? adventurer? explorer? businessman or businesswoman?
family member proceeding to an occasion, happy or sad?

Now we're going to go figure

In the city of music stands a fountain of pitches

Was it not as heroic at a very young age to have died as at a very old age to
have survived

The sun burns every story to a crisp and leaves only a lisp, or lapse, palsy, panic,
or a princess pointing at something across another now

Thrown onto the land, set loose on the ground, put precipitously in place, a person
of modern times will have many modern memories—but not just those

Why is there no one instead of someone

Watch out, you almost let yourself follow

The sociable book is ample and uninhibited, unashamed of its jolly
idiosyncrasies, unembarrassed by its infuriated sentimentality—o lucky
sociable book off the shelf

Distribute, puzzle, soap a rabbit, link anxieties, follow politics, toe snow

Survival can't wait

70

Resolute as the canyon oak, she branches, then leaves
A hit can indicate an accidental interest or a very real interest but at a distance
She breathes glances
Call her a poet at a podium, tolerate fate with pandemonium, savor the sweet
There are some who must do what they do with harm
A novella is not a plump story though it might be of people in chairs
Order is preserved as citron, a unit of value, a curl in increasing sugar
This cannot blunt the point of the parallel between a cough and a thought, or
       there is no parallel
I can't run away from you, I can't, says the gingerbread man in the end, if there
       were one
I will say that sleep is political
Anise pleasures, sponge delights, gravitational merriment—these are those
Patches are things to sigh into sutured inches
Let us remember a woman who exercised luscious wonder, let us remember a
       man with a circumspect camera
Are you atop a word hill, a lexical mappa mundi, and do you know us

In memory of Hillary Gravendyk

71

A grasshopper singing of death laughs long—as if a heavy-hearted granny spoke a
  light word
A shadow scuds over glass, the glass stands still
Insects seethe and they say *that* is the dream of language but what is language if
  not what is threading through the veins of an insect's wings
What does it mean to say "now" now, as now surfaces in a gesture, as of a person
  pushing his eyeglasses up toward his brow
Our luggage is stacked sky-high, we are wearing twenty layers of clothes, every
  utterance is symphonic
I've never made curtains for these windows, stabbed by the mid-morning light
I pass with a broom, standing with a hose in my hand and my thumb against the nozzle
The loops of time droop, fall slack—and someone steps out of those that were his
  or hers, hers or his, his and hers, his and his, hers and hers—is it right,
  then, that we are left to hurtle alone
The girls danced in dead light, the cadavers lay in live light—but as for those girls,
  men with mouths like mare vaginas watched them
Every rough rupture demands elasticity of the imagination
The silver river is irreversible but you attentively watch its mouth
What you write achieves its independence though you are nimble, arrogant, sly and wise
That is how you spend the day, which is itself a powerful force and raises the
  significant question "How did you get here?"
All suffering is in the egg—now suck it out of its shell and spit it away

In memoriam Arkadii Trofimovich Dragomoshchenko
February 3 1946-September 12, 2012

72

Collective longer literature appeals to cloud variants over a crowd
See the gang, going to Alabama, tonguing cones, singing waka wasa bong
The robust thrush it is, stately as royalty, common as a pickpocket at a concert
I will not, I say, rest, I say, rotate
Let's go now to the very next neologism and term it fragmentarily
Desperate he was to cry out and couldn't, to say what he knew and know it
This takes adults—and very far indeed
The saxophonist breathes, takes a breath, inhales, gasps
Armadillo, yellow shovel, and empty oval
I sprawl across a bed strewn with breadcrumbs, ah ha
At echo's edge, a rock wall rises, a monument to leisure
The mourner chortles, she's like a clown with sandpaper, at sorrow's involuntary humor
Her remarks, his remarks, their remarks, our remarks, my remarks, your remarks
      betray
O, there is a blading in this gentle bend

73

Listen up

Feelings of panic, preference for red meat or leafy greens, longing for nocturnal silence and dark—now find out just how human all that is

If a person dreams of one goldfish it means that he or she will have holes in his or her socks by the end of the following day, if he or she dreams of many goldfish it means nothing

I will now pursue a corpuscular trajectory, up and around and down and up

But let the fiddle scream / And be ye happy

Spinoza says we have "a monstrous lust of each to crush the other"

Pillage, pilfer, weep, digress

You may blame malaise on the weather, but be sure it's your own malaise

There's a logic of shipping, a logic of sails, and a churn-gaited, flat-footed logic of travel

I know what I do and this is it—well, I think so—I won't ask if I'm doing it here

You can't rehearse memory, you can't rehearse the future

Hand in the air—wing to dirt: wing wins

Carlotta Priscilla Jones scissors smoke, Megan Mary Lamartine boots salad, Lisa Leslie Lily Blake canoes laughs, and—as a bovine crow—Lyn Hejinian lows

The earth's surface is made

74

She stilled cream-colored stones an eternity ago and one bird flying there too
This is a pictograph of sediment not sentiment, of unbound layers of mud not
       the sold ore of South African gold
It is said that seven sleepers slumbered for two centuries and then woke up
The dead have mixed
Writers dowse in books, and being one I find that the first two words on page
       203 of the book are Wilfred Owen's (bent double) and the first two on
       page 307 are Auden's (amid rustle)—magic
What might a demographer dare
Behold the scooters and riders and divers, scooting and riding and diving up
The young woman on tiptoe said and we didn't doubt
What's desirable then isn't writable—there are more walls than trees there
Clerk, haven't you a pen with pigs in it
Okay, I'm leaning back, as if that would help me remember from pungency and
       acerbic comments relegating Natasha Rostov to the makeshift stages of
       a sitcom, but I fall—off that stage
Butter jumps
Curmudgeon
The autobiographical isn't renewable—so who is she

75

During the later years of my war, you were a middle soldier in the army of the metronome
Do not say she was my bother, parting ways, o mother of my brother
Let's go to bed to lie to ourselves leadenly in leisure
Mars, melody, pigeons in a laundry basket, and a little dancer's body knowledge
Whatever
Word hover
I've got my black look on, but it's wearing thin white cat hairs
Appearance of the world, disappearance of coherence
The empty page provides a preparatory pleasure, or, perhaps, it instigates a
     preparatory desire
I have sharpened the carmine and vermillion, I could plunge through the hole in
     my tongue, but I think, and then I bellow
I ask myself, what is argon, and tell myself, it is a noble gas, just as argot is ignoble
     speech, the can-your-ass of those who can
Si se puedes, the strikers chant
In the night sky, dimmer than the Pleiades, stretch the strings of the stars' guitar
Canvas bourgeois zero

76

One day a woman I'll name another day hitched her pelicans to a raft and went
   to sea
Every day, all the way—wheel it
Unless one gets the picture, one can't get the caption
So I was in the tree, one foot in the air, and it was there, as I sucked juice from a
   lemon through a peppermint stick, that I saw the dinner guests arrive
Fluorescent navy flowers, incandescent sand buttons, and militant blazing
   fireflies—yes or no
As a rider of a city bus I am in the early morning light at the window a fly, or, as
   a fly I am a city rider at a window in the early bus light
Windows walkway leaves to abandon
As a bow-shaped bird of prey she hovers as an inclination in its freedom
Damage is not the same as discontent but may elicit insincerity rather than
   sarcasm, perplexity rather than allegories
Whizzing samurai shuttlecocks
I am open to jeremiads
One winter's evening on wheels dreary the human face flapped its feet
A great gaseous ghost is growing in a notch, it sleeps below the telephone lines
   that send ideas between ears
Have you never filled potatoes with bitter butter

77

I have had responsibility land somewhere and irresponsibility fly like a dark eagle
  after a golden cat
Right again: a spill of M & M's
A grape is a stone for a long turn of a clock or a stone is a grape in a sock
What is love but imagination
Willing syrup regent cap nut father, Father
Then the capricious zebra zolted, janglishly, carpet-riding
Did she not yearn, would she not have yearned, couldn't she have yearned—she
  will have yearned but won't yearn
The very grandmothers with stones in their hearts press the lightness of the sound
  of crickets nicking laughter, lacking shadow-casters
In name I am a slipper, strengthened by circular calcium
Heliophiles leap toward the dawn, heliophiles saddle butter
I've no other sentence to speak, to syntax, to serve
Be vigilant, Virgil
A stricken statistician leaps blue concrete—can we see the numberless trail and travail
Suns go

Notes

15: "We cannot hope to continue indefinitely without ever getting into trouble": See H. O. Mounce, *Wittgenstein's Tractatus: An Introduction*, 123.

17: "E appears more often than T, T more often than A, A more often than I": See John Lyons, *Semantics* I (43).

22: "The very fact of pointing to something commits the person who is pointing to the conviction that there is something there / to the existence of what she's pointing at": See John Lyons, *Semantics*, vol II, 656.

36: The phrase "Girls, my anchor has run out of print" : John Schott

39: "Voyage in place: that is the name of all intensities" : Gilles Deleuze and Félix Guattari, *A Thousand Plateaus*, 482.

46: "In due course anti-lions and anti-asps will befriend wandering humans on sailing ships propelled by calm": Walter Benjamin, *The Arcades Project*, W1a, 622.

55: "As for memory, it…is much closer to knowledge than to life": Eugene Minkowski, *Lived Time: Phenomenlogical and Psychopathological Studies*, 80, quoted in Elizabeth Grosz, "Thinking the New: Of Futures Yet Unthought," in Elizabeth Grosz, ed., *Becomings: Explorations in Time, Memory, and Futures* (Ithaca: Cornell University Press, 1999), 21.

56: "By moving from window to window and carefully recording at each what we see, we…": Almost a direct quote from David Harvey, *The Limits to Capital* (London & NY: Verso, 2006), 2.

73: "But let the fiddle scream / And be ye happy": Wordsworth, *The Prelude*, Book II, 40-41.

73: "Spinoza says we have 'a monstrous lust of each to crush the other'": Spinoza, *Ethics*, IVP58.

Lyn Hejinian is a poet, essayist, teacher, and translator. Her academic work is addressed principally to modernist, postmodern, and contemporary poetry and poetics, with a particular interest in avant-garde movements and the social practices they entail. She is the co-director (with Travis Ortiz) of *Atelos*, a literary project commissioning and publishing cross-genre work by poets. In addition to her literary and academic work, she has in recent years been involved in anti-privatization activism at the University of California, Berkeley, where she serves as the John F. Hotchkis Professor of English.

Cover art by Sofie Ramos ©2015
www.sofieramos.com.

Born in Cincinnati, Ohio in 1990, she received a BA in Visual Art from Brown University in 2013 and her MFA in Art Practice at UC Berkeley in 2015. She lives and works in Oakland, California.

PROCESS NOTE:
Like Lyn's approach to the poems in *The Unfollowing*, my artistic process uses decidedly illogical progression to interrogate the perceived stability of what might be logical, where those boundaries can break down, how they reincarnate. The improvisational and inconclusive process of accumulating, arranging, reusing and reworking layers of visual material reveals an underlying tension in the fluidity of formal and psychological oppositions. What was logical starts to seem nonsensical; pleasure accelerates into nausea; ordered systems become chaotic; alternative systems of logic and order emerge, unfamiliar forms of pleasure. What was essential to the structure of the composition becomes excess; the question of what's essential becomes inessential. Symbols break down into disjointed, meaningless fragments; new, ambiguous symbols appear. A core concern of the work resides in the shifting relationships determined by the juxtaposition of elements rather than in the identity of each or the overall object/space they compose.

The Unfollowing
by Lyn Hejinian

Cover text set in Trajan Pro, Garamond 3 LT Std, and Perpetua Std
Interior text set in Garamond 3 LT Std

Cover art by Sofie Ramos ©2015
www.sofieramos.com.

Cover and interior design by Cassandra Smith

Omnidawn Publishing
Richmond, California
2016

Rusty Morrison & Ken Keegan, senior editors & co-publishers
Gillian Olivia Blythe Hamel, managing editor
Melissa Burke, marketing manager
Cassandra Smith, poetry editor & book designer
Peter Burghardt, poetry editor & book designer
Sharon Zetter, poetry editor, book designer & development officer
Liza Flum, poetry editor & marketing assistant
Juliana Paslay, fiction editor
Gail Aronson, fiction editor
RJ Ingram, *OmniVerse* contributing editor
Kevin Peters, marketing assistant & *OmniVerse* Lit Scene editor
Trisha Peck, marketing assistant
Sara Burant, administrative assistant
Josie Gallup, publicity assistant
SD Sumner, publicity assistant

Publication of this book was made possible in part by gifts from:
Robin & Curt Caton
John Gravendyk